How Is Maple Syrup Made?

by Grace Hansen

Abdo Kids Jumbo is an Imprint of Abdo Kids
abdobooks.com

abdobooks.com

Published by Abdo Kids, a division of ABDO, P.O. Box 398166, Minneapolis, Minnesota 55439.

Abdo Kids Jumbo™ is a trademark and logo of Abdo Kids.

102018

012019

Photo Credits: iStock, Shutterstock

Production Contributors: Teddy Borth, Jennie Forsberg, Grace Hansen

Design Contributors: Dorothy Toth, Laura Mitchell

Library of Congress Control Number: 2018945977

Publisher's Cataloging-in-Publication Data

Names: Hansen, Grace, author.

Title: How is maple syrup made? / by Grace Hansen.

Description: Minneapolis, Minnesota : Abdo Kids, 2019 | Series: How is it made?
Includes glossary, index and online resources (page 24).

Identifiers: ISBN 9781532181955 (lib. bdg.) | ISBN 9781532182938 (ebook) |
ISBN 9781532183423 (Read-to-me ebook)

Subjects: LCSH: Maple syrup--Juvenile literature. | Manufacturing processes--
Juvenile literature. | Maple syrup industry--Juvenile literature.

Classification: DDC 664.13--dc23

Table of Contents

O Canada!

Maple syrup is made from the **sap** in maple trees. There are maple trees in the United States. But the largest ones grow in Canada!

Tap for Sap

A worker drills a hole into a maple tree. Then the worker hammers a **tap** into the hole. **Sap** seeps into the tap.

The **taps** are connected to a large network of trees and pipes. The pipes run downhill. The **sap** flows through the pipes and into a large bin.

At the Plant

A maple tree's **sap** is thin and watery. It is taken to an **evaporation** plant.

At the plant, the **sap** is put into a large tank. The sap is heated to more than 200 degrees F (93°C). The heat causes water to **evaporate**.

This process takes several hours. The temperature must remain steady. And the **sap** is watched closely. If the sap is heated for too long, it could **crystallize**.

F
260
240
220
200
180
160
140

When enough water has evaporated, the tank is drained. The fresh, hot syrup is filtered through cotton.

The syrup is ready for bottling!

Pure maple syrup is often sold in small bottles. It is expensive to buy. But it is worth it!

More Facts

- It takes about 40 liters (10.6 g) of tree **sap** to make 1 liter (.26 g) of maple syrup.
- The youngest maple tree that can be **tapped** is 40 years old.
- The first written account of humans eating a maple tree's sap is from 1606.

Glossary

crystallize – to change into crystals.

evaporate – to turn from liquid into gas.

filter – to go through a filter so that any solids are removed from a liquid.

sap – a watery and sugary solution that runs through a plant.

tap – a device to control the flow of liquid.

Index

Visit **abdokids.com** and use this code to access crafts, games, videos, and more!